# Contents

Words in **bold** are explained in the glossary.

# What is a map?

A map is a special drawing. This drawing is usually of an area as seen from above.

This area can be as big as the world. Or it can be as small as a classroom in your school!

# USING MAPS

# Our environment

by Susan Hoe

ticktock

913 000 00024473

**By Susan Hoe**
**Series consultant: Debra Voege**
**Editor: Mark Sachner**
**Project manager: Joe Harris**
***ticktock* designer: Hayley Terry**
**Picture research: Lizzie Knowles and Joe Harris**

Copyright © 2008 ticktock Entertainment Ltd.
First published in Great Britain by ticktock Media Ltd.,
The Old Sawmill, 103 Goods Station Road, Tunbridge Wells, Kent TN1 2DP, Great Britain.

A CIP catalogue record for this book is available from the British Library.

ISBN 978 1 84696 914 0

Printed in China

PICTURE CREDITS

China Images/ Alamy: 17tl. Victor Englebert/ photographersdirect.com: 20t, 21t. Getmapping PLC: 24c. Sean Harris: 4b, 8. iStock: 4t, 6t, 7b, 11tr, 11c, 12t, 12b, 19tl, 22t, 25b. Jupiter Images: 2. Lehtikuva Oy/ Rex Features: 19tr. Oliver Polet/ Corbis: 17b. Ulli Seer/ Getty Images: 5t. Shutterstock: 6b, 11tl, 11b, 15bl, 15br, 17tr, 18b, 19b, 24tl, 24b, 25t, 25c. Justin Spain: 4c, 9 all, 21b, 31t. Hayley Terry: 5b, 10, 13 all, 15t, 19c, 27, 30. Tim Thirlaway: 28, 29. Time and Life Pictures/ Getty Images: 20b. www.mapart.co.uk: 7t, 14, 16, 18, 22b, 23, 26, 31b.

# Making a map of an island

## Map Key

 Trees/woods

 Roads/footpaths

 Grey-roofed buildings

Red-roofed buildings

 Piers

 Gardens

Maps help us find things as if we were directly above them.

In this book, we will learn about some ways that maps tell us about the environment. But first let's look at some of the ways that maps help us.

**Find the biggest building in the photo of the island.**

**Now find it on the map.**

# Why do we need maps?

*Maps help us find our way around. They give us all kinds of information about where we live.*

A map can help you get from one place to another. It can show you where you are, where you want to go, and how to get there.

**Weather map of the UK and Ireland**

This map shows you what the weather will be like where you live.

**Can you tell what kinds of weather this map is showing?**

## Map of the world

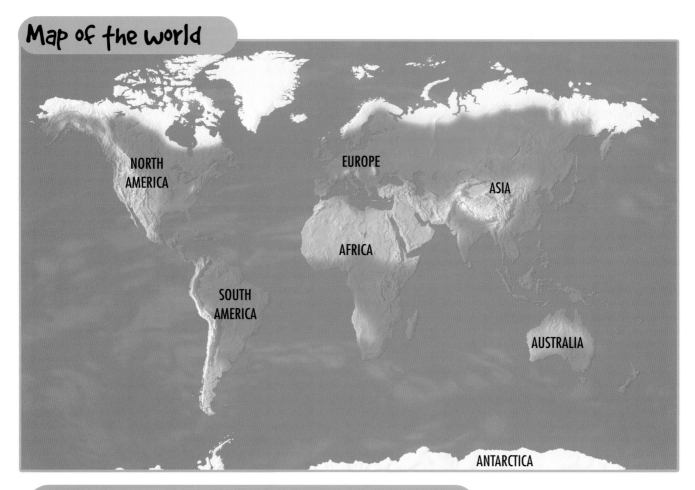

NORTH AMERICA

EUROPE

ASIA

AFRICA

SOUTH AMERICA

AUSTRALIA

ANTARCTICA

**This map shows the world's deserts in yellow. The forests and woods are in green. Places covered in snow and ice are white.**

Maps teach us important facts about places. These places might be close to home or on the other side of the world.

Maps show us whether the land is flat or hilly. They can show us where people and animals live. We can also learn what crops are grown and what sorts of things are made in a place.

Maps are handy and easy to use. They can show us huge areas in a small amount of space. We can take them just about anywhere!

# Mapping your classroom

*Maps show how a place seems if you are looking down on it. That place can be your country or your town. It can even be a classroom in your school!*

A 3-D classroom

This classroom is a **three-dimensional (3-D)** space. The room and things in the room are solid. They have length, width, and **depth**.

# A 2-D map

A map is a **two-dimensional (2-D)** drawing of a space. Everything in the classroom now looks flat.

To create a 2-D map of this classroom, we draw all the flat shapes on a piece of paper.

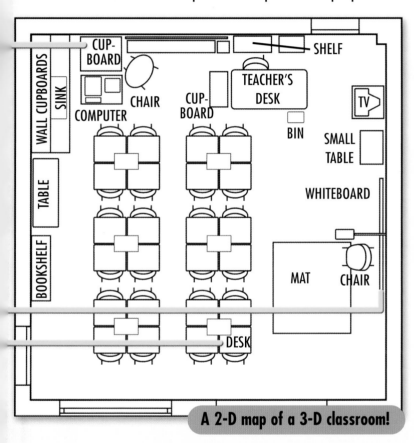

WALL CUPBOARDS
SINK
COMPUTER
CUP-BOARD
CHAIR
TABLE
BOOKSHELF
SHELF
TEACHER'S DESK
CUP-BOARD
TV
BIN
SMALL TABLE
WHITEBOARD
MAT
CHAIR
DESK

**A 2-D map of a 3-D classroom!**

This map shows you how to find everything in the classroom.

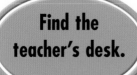
**Find the teacher's desk.**

**Find the shelves.**

## Making the map

This drawing of the classroom was made from the photograph.

Pretend you are able to float up above the room and look down on it.

When you are right above the room, it looks flat. This is the view we use to make a 2-D map.

# Mapping a place for a new school

*A new school needs lots of land to be built on. It must have a school building, car park, and playground. To run smoothly, the school needs special **services** from the town.*

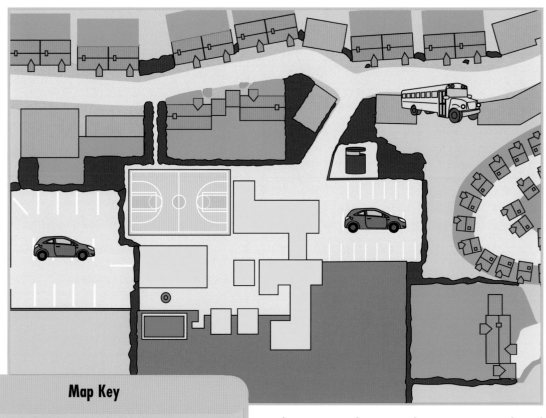

## Map Key

| | | | |
|---|---|---|---|
| Car park | | Shops | |
| Playground | | Water fountain | |
| Bus stop | | Hedge | |
| Rubbish bins | | Gardens | |
| School building | | School playing field | |
| Residential homes | | Swimming pool | |

This map shows what a new school needs. It uses different symbols to identify each thing. The map has a key. This **map key** is also called a legend. It tells you what each symbol stands for.

**Find the playground.**

**Find the bus stop.**

## Town services

Towns provide many services that schools need.

The electrical plant supplies all the electricity.

A town **reservoir** holds the water used in the school. This reservoir is formed by a large **dam**.

New roads are built so that students can get to school.

The rubbish is taken to the city dump. Some items are taken to a **recycling** plant.

# Changes in your town's environment

*When a new building goes up, it causes changes in the area.*

A new school can mean more classrooms and better student equipment.

A new school can also cause traffic jams, however. More traffic can mean more air **pollution** from cars.

## Making good choices for the environment

The town of Summerton needs a new hospital. You must decide where to build it. Look at this map of Summerton and the two hospital plans. Which plan would you choose? Which one would be better for the town's **environment** and harm fewer fields, forests and lakes? Why?

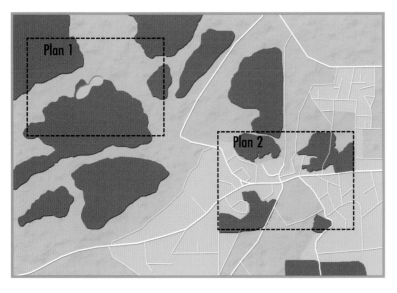

**Map Key**

| | |
|---|---|
| | Field |
| | Forest |
| | Lake |
| | Road |
| | Town |
| | Proposed site |

## Plan 1

The hospital will be built in a wooded area far from town. There are no roads around. Trees must be cut down and the pond emptied and filled in with soil to make more building space. A cement car park will be built.

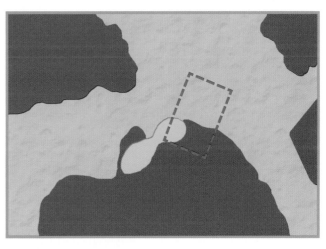

## Plan 2

The hospital will be built in a field that is near a main road. More trees will be planted around the building. A car park will be built under the ground. It will not be seen from the road.

# Changes in our country's environment

*You can show more than just the streets of your home town on a map. In fact you can show the roads of a whole country! Roads let people and **goods** move across the United Kingdom.*

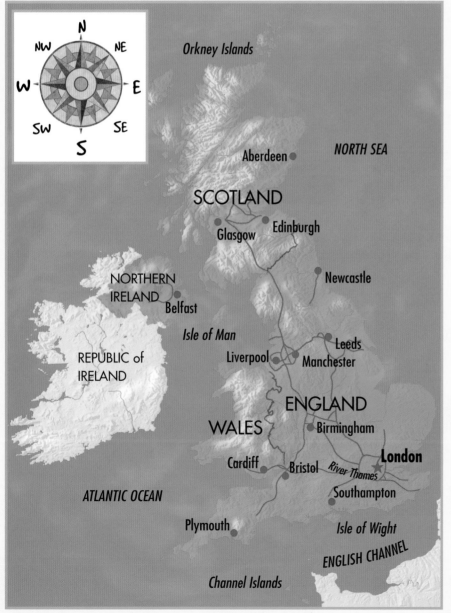

This map shows the most important roads in the United Kingdom, called motorways. They go through cities, fields, mountains, coastal areas, and even over waterways. Some go east and west. Some travel north to south. Many cross over each other.

The **compass rose** at the top left of this map shows you which direction is north (N), south (S), east (E), or west (W). It may also show northeast (NE), southeast (SE), southwest (SW), and northwest (NW).

Over many years, people have built roads, bridges, airports, and railways across the United Kingdom.

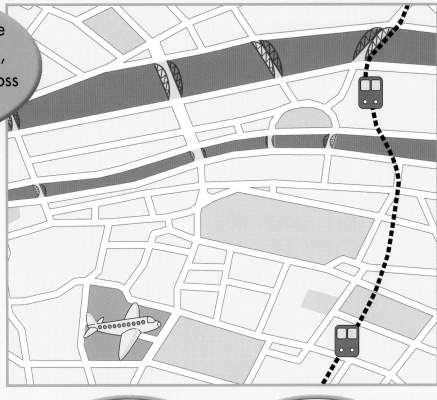

### Map Key

Bridge

Railway track

Airport

Road

River

Parkland

This city map shows many roads and man-made **structures**.

**Find a bridge.**

**Find the railway track.**

## on the road

Clean roads and motorways help us to protect the environment. They also protect the natural beauty of an area.

Roads take people to their destinations. Be kind to the environment when travelling by car.

Travel with litter bags to store your rubbish. Empty them when you have reached your destination.

# Where do people live around the world?

*Most people gather where there is water and food. They also want safe roads and ways to get to shops and other locations. When many people live in a place, they make a big impact on their environment.*

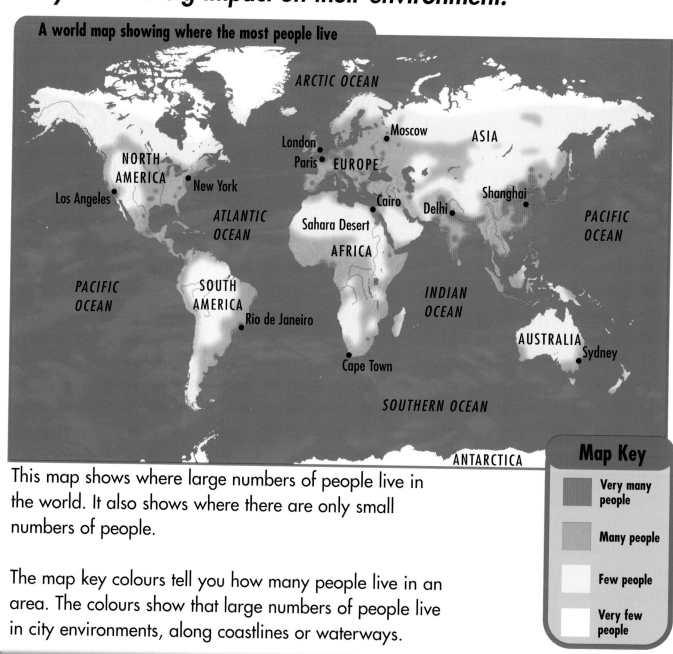

A world map showing where the most people live

ARCTIC OCEAN

Moscow

ASIA

London
Paris • EUROPE

NORTH AMERICA • New York

Los Angeles •

ATLANTIC OCEAN

Cairo

Delhi •

Shanghai •

PACIFIC OCEAN

Sahara Desert

AFRICA

PACIFIC OCEAN

SOUTH AMERICA

• Rio de Janeiro

INDIAN OCEAN

AUSTRALIA

Sydney

Cape Town

SOUTHERN OCEAN

ANTARCTICA

**Map Key**

Very many people

Many people

Few people

Very few people

This map shows where large numbers of people live in the world. It also shows where there are only small numbers of people.

The map key colours tell you how many people live in an area. The colours show that large numbers of people live in city environments, along coastlines or waterways.

The Sahara Desert in Africa has very little natural water. Therefore, very few people live there.

Shanghai is a city in China. It has a big seaport. For humans, it is one of the most crowded environments in the world.

## Fighting pollution

People are the cause of most pollution in the world. But people also help solve many pollution problems. **Governments** and groups like **UNICEF** are working to clean up the environment.

The new well in this African village has been built by UNICEF.

# A rainforest environment

**Rainforests** *are areas of land with thick plant growth. Millions of animals live there, too. Some living things in Earth's rainforests are still waiting to be discovered!*

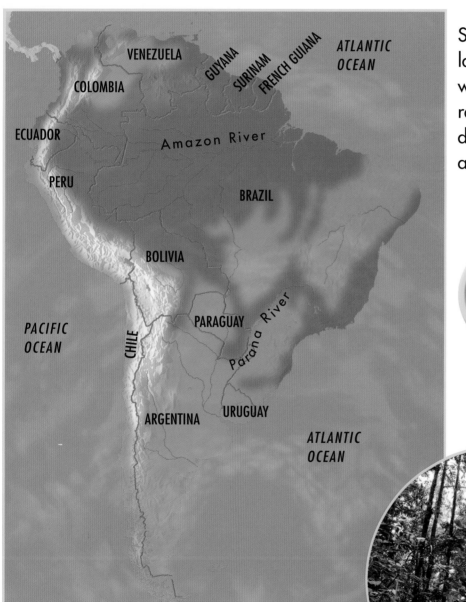

South America has the largest rainforests in the world. On this map, the rainforests are shown as dark green. The countries are outlined in red.

**In which South American country is the most rainforest found?**

Heavy rainfall keeps the rainforest thick and green. Many rare plants from rainforests are used to make medicines.

The rainforests are shrinking.
Too many trees are being cut down.
This process is called 'deforestation'.

The harpy eagle is in danger of becoming **extinct**.

When so many trees are cut down, many rainforest animals lose their homes and die out.

## Deforestation of a rainforest area

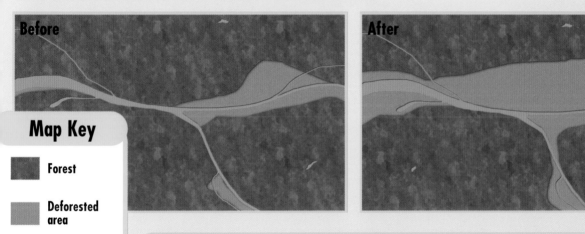

Before

After

### Map Key

Forest

Deforested area

River

These 'before' and 'after' maps show how much of this rainforest has disappeared.

## How can you help?

Paper is made from wood. Try to recycle paper so fewer trees are cut down to make new paper. When you buy paper, look for the symbol on the right. It means the paper is recycled.

People are working to save rainforests and the animals that live there.

# Mapping a rainforest village

**The rainforest of Brazil is home to different groups of people. One such group is the Yanomami tribe.**

This is Shoco, a young Yanomami boy. He and his family live with other families not far from a river. Their way of life is in danger from deforestation.

The Yanomamis eat fish that they catch from their canoes on the river. They also eat meat from the animals they hunt in the rainforest.

Shoco and his family sleep in hammocks that are hung inside their house.

The tribe gathers nuts and fruits in the rainforest. They also grow sweet potatoes and plantains (a type of banana) in their gardens.

The Yanomamis live all together in a large doughnut-shaped house called a shabono.

This map of a Yanomami home uses symbols that stand for different parts of the house. The map key helps you understand what the symbols mean.

Map of Shoco's home

**Map Key**

| | |
|---|---|
| ⬯ | Hammock |
| ✳ | Fireplace |
| ▦ | Shelving |
| ● | Post |
| ✿ | Tall tree |
| ▥ | Roof |
| ▨ | Rainforest |

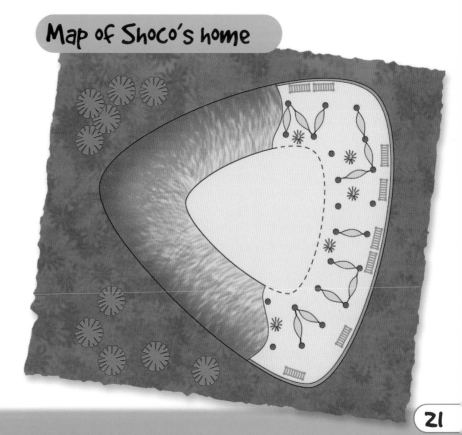

# Drawing maps

*Before you can draw a map, you must figure out the exact size and shape of the mapping area. This means figuring out how to measure large areas.*

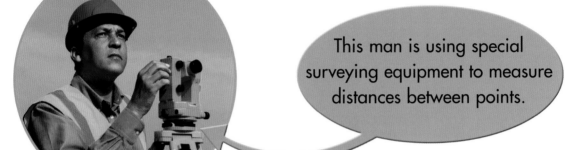

This man is using special surveying equipment to measure distances between points.

Mapmakers use their measurements to draw their maps. The maps on these pages show the attractions at an amusement park.

## Scale: shrinking to fit

When mapmakers have gathered all their measurements, they must figure out how to fit them onto a piece of paper. So they shrink, or scale down, the real measurements to make a map.

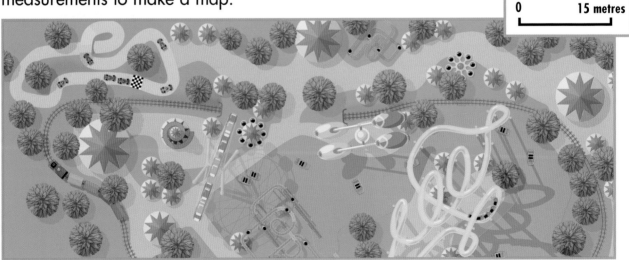

This small-scaled map shows a fairly large area. Many objects are visible, but they are quite small.

Different scales used to map the same area change what you see. Small-scale maps show large areas on a sheet of paper. Large-scale maps show smaller areas, but the objects look bigger and have more detail.

The map **scale** tells you how long a metre is on the map. This way you can figure out real distances on the map.

0     8 metres

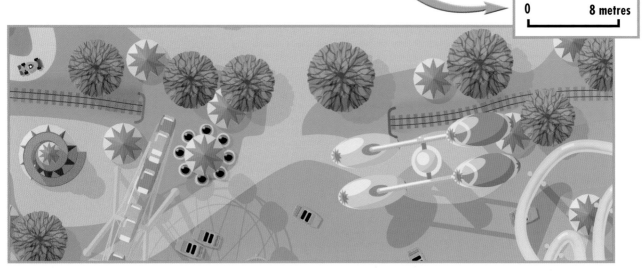

This larger-scaled map shows a smaller area than the first map. The map scale also shows that each centimetre is equal to fewer metres. So you see fewer objects on this map, but you can see them in greater detail.

0     5 metres

This map has the largest scale. It shows an even smaller area. You see even fewer objects, but you can see them in even greater detail.

# Hi-tech mapmaking

*Many years ago, people used their travels to figure out the shape of the land. Today, mapmakers use new, hi-tech equipment.*

**Mapmakers can take many photographs of the ground from a plane.**

This photograph shows the ground below as seen from the plane.

The pictures and measurements taken from the plane are sent to computers that draw a map.

Mapmakers also use satellites to take pictures of Earth from space.

A satellite orbiting Earth.

The pictures taken by these satellites are beamed back to Earth. They are put together to make pictures of our planet, like the one shown here. These pictures can then be turned into maps.

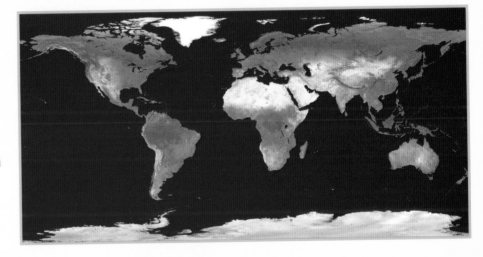

## Ever-changing maps

Satellites can tell where your car is on the road. They can produce road maps that help you find your destination. These maps constantly change as you need them. The maps are called GPS, or Global Positioning System, maps.

A GPS map at work in a car.

# Mapping natural disasters in South America

Natural disasters are sudden events like earthquakes or hurricanes, which cause great damage to a place.

- Volcanic eruption 1985
- Hurricane 1968, 1996
- Hurricane 1968, 1996
- Earthquake 1949
- Earthquake 1970
- Wildfire 1998
- Earthquake 2007
- Tsunami 1868, 1960
- Earthquake 1939
- Hurricane 2004
- Tornado 1973
- Earthquake 1944

South America has had many natural disasters. Here's a way to map out these events from the past.

## Making a map of natural disasters

1. Copy the map of South America on page 26 onto a blank sheet of paper. You could also use a thin piece of tracing paper to trace the map.

2. Now make a map key. Draw symbols on it to represent earthquakes, volcanic eruptions, tsunamis, hurricanes, tornadoes and wildfires.

3. The map on page 26 shows where each of these natural disasters happened. Use this map key as a guide to draw your own natural disaster pictures on your map of South America. Be sure to draw the natural disaster symbols so they look like the ones in your map key.

## Map Key

Earthquake: a strong shaking of the ground.

Volcanic eruptions: when hot lava from inside the earth bursts out of a volcano.

Tsunami (tidal wave): a destructive giant wave, caused by an earthquake under the ocean.

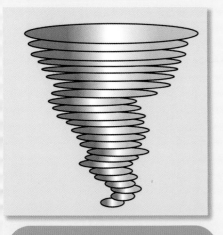

Tornado: a funnel-shaped wind that can pick up heavy objects.

Wildfire: a very bad fire that spreads quickly through forested areas.

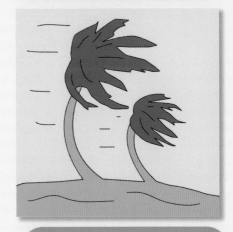

Hurricane: a strong storm with high winds and heavy rains.

# Making a map of your own beach

*A beach is a fun natural environment to visit. Why not make your own beach map? Make a map key too so your friends can find all the great things in it.*

What kind of shape will your beach be? Circle, oval, crescent, rectangle?

How many lifeguard stations will it have? Where will they be placed?

Alex's Amazing Beach

What fun things can people do at your beach? Will there be a pier for fishing, paddleboats, an ice cream stall, or a crazy golf course?

Does your beach have public toilets, outdoor showers, a car park, or a first aid station?

## Step 1

Draw the shape of your beach on a piece of paper. Is it on an ocean or a lakefront?

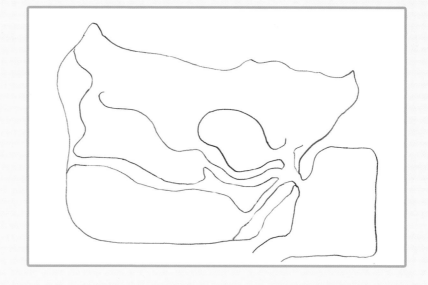

## Step 2

Make up different symbols for all the beach items you want to include on your map. Be sure you leave enough space between all the different symbols. Draw in the sandy beach area, any grassy areas, and car parks.

## Step 3

Colour your beach map, and give the beach a name.

## Step 4

Make your map key using the symbols on your map.

Water    Shower    Food stall    Crazy golf

Pier    Sand    Public toilets    Parking

Lifeguard tower    Water fountain    First aid    Rowing boats hire

Grass    Rubbish bin    Picnic area    Play area

# Glossary

**Compass rose:** a drawing that shows directions on a map: north (N), south (S), east (E) and west (W).

**Dam**: a concrete wall that holds back water.

**Depth**: the length from the top of a space or an object to its bottom.

**Environment:** the area and space where people, plants, and animals live.

**Equipment:** tools and other items used for a specific job.

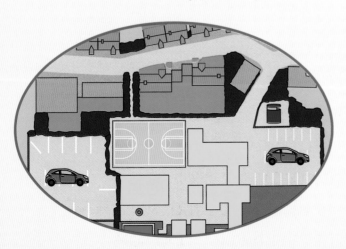

**Extinct:** when a kind of animal has died out, and none are alive any more.

**Goods:** items that people grow or make. People can buy and sell goods.

**Governments:** the groups of people who make the laws and rule in a country or area.

**Map key:** the space on a map that shows the meaning of any pictures or colours used on the map.

**Pollution:** unclean things found in the air, soil, and water.

**Rainforests:** large wooded areas with lots of warm rainfall that produce big trees and shrubs. Little sunlight gets through the thick growth of trees.

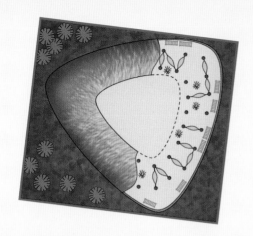

**Recycling:** turning rubbish into something that can be used again – especially cans, glass, plastic, and paper.

**Reservoir:** a place where fresh water is collected and stored for people to use.

**Scale:** the amount by which the measurement of an area is shrunk to fit on a map. The map scale is a drawing or symbol that tells how to measure distances on a map.

**Services:** needed and useful help offered to people living in an area. Some services are rubbish disposal, recycling, water, and electricity.

**Structures:** buildings and other large man-made objects.

**Three-dimensional (3-D):** appearing as a solid thing that has length, width, and depth.

**Two-dimensional (2-D):** appearing as a flat shape with only length and width.

**UNICEF:** United Nations International Children's Emergency Fund (now called simply United Nations Children's Fund); a group that helps keep children healthy and safe.

# Index